EB-5 AND U.S. SECURITIES LAW

PART ONE

Chapter One: Regulation D Offerings; Now is the Time

Chapter Two: EB-5 Visas: Pitfalls and Benefits of U.S. Securities Laws

Chapter Three: Direct Investments versus regional centers

PART TWO

Chapter Four: Business Brokers Acting as Broker-Dealers and/or Underwriters

Chapter Five: Brokers, Dealers and Finders

Chapter Six: Purchaser Representatives

PART THREE

Chapter Seven: EB-5 Law and Practice Post JOBS Act

Chapter Eight: Implementing the JOBS Act

PART FOUR

Chapter Nine: The Regulation S Option

Chapter Ten: Sample Regulation S Disclaimer Language

About the author

Web sites and blogs that Douglas Slain has managed for the last several years include **PrivatePlacementAdvisors.com, RegDConsumersReport.com** and **RegDLaw.com.** Books he has written include *Real Estate Blind Pools* and *Delivery Services.*

Doug is the manager of a LinkedIn discussion group focusing on state securities enforcement and private placement law with over 1250 members, **Securities Enforcement and Regulation.** He has served as an expert witness in litigation involving compliance with Regulation D and private placement law.

Doug was the founding editor and long term publisher of *Insurance Litigation Reporter, Professional Liability Reporter, Medical Liability Reporter,* and *Construction Litigation Reporter,* titles now published by Thomson-Reuters. More recently, he was the publisher of *Securities Enforcement Reporter* and *Blue Sky Chronicle.* His first job out of college was as a reporter for *The Wall Street Journal.*

Doug practiced real estate and finance law at Pillsbury, Madison & Sutro and later served as a rule of law consultant to the Ministry of Economy for the Republic of Latvia as its secured transactions adviser. He taught one semester at Stanford Law School as an adjunct clinical law professor. He served as chairman of the American Bar Association's Professional Responsibility Committee for two terms.

Doug received a JD from Stanford Law School, a MA from the University of Chicago, a BA from DePauw University, a diploma from University College London, and a certificate from the Goethe Institute.

PART ONE

Chapter One: Regulation D Offerings: Now is the Time

$1 Trillion/Annum Set to Increase to At Least $2 trillion

Proceeds from Regulation D private offerings have totaled almost $1 trillion in recent years despite a regulatory scheme that prohibited the use of general solicitation or general advertising. Now that regulatory scheme is set to change dramatically, and up to $2 trillion per year is possible.

Section 201(a) (1) of the JOBS Act directs the SEC to modify Rule 506 under Regulation D to remove the general solicitation prohibition in offerings where all investors are accredited investors.

The new rule provides a securities registration exemption for private offerings that use general solicitation or general advertising, provided all purchasers are accredited investors and reasonable steps to verify accredited investor status are taken.

A SEC release indicates certain circumstances that will tend to require fewer – or more – verifying steps, including:

1. Nature of the purchaser and type of accredited investor the purchaser claims to be;
2. Amount and type of information the issuer has about a purchaser;
3. Nature of the offering, such as the manner in which the purchaser was solicited (mass media, internet or pre-screened data base of wealthy clients of broker dealer);
4. Terms of the offering, such as a large minimum investment amount; and

5. Financing purchaser's large cash investment by the issuer or a third party.

Under Regulation D an investor is treated as an accredited investor if one of two conditions is satisfied if the issuer "reasonably believes" the investor met such requirements.

The SEC recently observed: "[W]e anticipate that many practices currently used by issuers [to establish reasonable belief] in connection with existing Rule 506 offerings would satisfy the verification requirement proposed for offerings pursuant to [New] Rule 506(c)."

The SEC did not endorse self-certification as a sufficient stand-alone verifying step for most offerings. The information that issuers must have about a prospective investor will not be limited solely to one checked box on a subscription agreement. However, the amount of information the issuer has about an investor may be significantly limited for prospective investors attracted to an offering through the internet or other mass media and with whom the issuer had no relationship before the offer.

In addition to criticizing self-certification, NASAA has recommended that the SEC adopt new non-exclusive "safe harbors" that will be deemed to be reasonable verification steps. NASAA suggested income should be verified by tax returns, Forms W-2 or 1099 or recent pay stubs. Some commentators have suggested that issuers and their advisers concerned about the absence of a safe-harbor will not rely on new Rule 506(c) as an effective capital raising exemption.

Some argue that the JOBS Act's language concerning reasonable steps to verify accredited investor status should not be made a substantive requirement of new Rule 506(c). The language regarding reasonable verifying steps directs the SEC to adopt rules requiring the issuer to take reasonable steps to verify accredited investor status. However, nothing in the language of the JOBS Act states that taking such reasonable verification steps is a condition of the new exemption.

The JOBS Act requires the SEC to adopt a rule directing issuers to use reasonable steps to verify accredited investor status, but the failure to undertake such steps does not necessarily result in a loss of the exemption. The existing provisions of Regulation D provide precedent for not losing an exemption for failure to follow rules requiring certain behavior. For example, Rule 503 requires the filing Form D, but failure to file the form will not destroy the availability of Regulation D for a transaction that otherwise satisfies applicable requirements of Regulation D.

Stay tuned for new developments. These developments are the most significant changes in private placement law in the last 30 years.

Chapter Two: EB-5 Visas: Pitfalls and Benefits of U.S. Securities Laws

The employment-creation immigrant visa category EB-5 has become the flavor of the month for wealthy foreign nationals, whether using a direct investment vehicle or a regional center. Many immigration lawyers praise the EB-5 regional center "pilot program" in particular as a simple means to both invest in the US and to obtain a green card. The purpose of this chapter is to discuss why prospective EB-5 investors should pay attention to the demands of Federal and state securities laws, whether using direct investment platforms or regional centers.

When a regional center or a direct investment entity forms a corporation, a limited partnership, or a limited liability company, the regional center or direct investment group is offering a security and, accordingly, must comply with Federal and state laws

WHY EB-5?

The EB-5 visa requires no anchor relative in the United States to petition on the immigrant's behalf. It requires no claim of extraordinary or exceptional ability. It also does not require a showing of fear of persecution in the homeland. This visa category instead allows conditional and permanent resident status by investing lawfully acquired funds (at least $500,000 within a rural area or one of high unemployment and $1 million anywhere else) in a regional center or direct investment entity approved by the U.S. Citizenship and Immigration Services (USCIS).The investor is provided a private placement memorandum and is asked to sign a subscription agreement. He will then be asked to deposit money into an escrow account.

WHY IS US SECURITIES LAW RELEVANT?

Foreign investors often have no idea that state and Federal securities laws exist to protect them by providing accurate information and to punish persons or entities that violate these laws. For instance, EB-5 investors must be told that not every investment is safe and not every investment in a regional center or direct investment will result in green card status, let alone produce a Profit

.

---

*The **Association of Southeast Asian Nations** (**ASEAN**) is a geo-political and economic organization of ten countries located in Southeast Asia, which was formed in 1967 by Indonesia, Malaysia, the Philippines, Singapore and Thailand. Since then, membership has expanded to include Brunei, Burma (Myanmar), Cambodia, Laos, and Vietnam. Its aims include accelerating economic growth, social progress, and cultural development among its members, protection of regional peace and stability, and opportunities for member countries to discuss differences peacefully.

WHAT IS A SECURITY?

The Securities Act of 1933, as amended (the "Securities Act"), defines "security" as any note, stock, bond, investment contract or any interest or instrument commonly known as a "security." The U.S. Securities and Exchange Commission ("SEC") has determined that interests in a limited partnership are an investment contract, and therefore, a security.

The Securities Act requires that all securities sold must be registered with the SEC, unless exempt. Rule 506 of Regulation D promulgated under the Securities Act sets forth the exemptions to the registration rules that regional centers and direct investment entities must use to avoid registration when soliciting EB-5 investor money.

To meet the exemptions provided by Regulation D, a regional center or direct investment entity must comply with the conditions set forth in Rule 502 of Regulation D, including information requirements. *If all of the investors are accredited investors, there are no informational requirements--although issuers of course are still subject to anti-fraud requirements.*

WHAT IS AN ACCREDITED INVESTOR?

An accredited investor is a person whose individual net worth, or joint net worth including that person's spouse, at the time of the purchase of the securities exceeds $1,000,000; or whose individual income exceeded $200,000 in each of the two most recent years (and who expects to reach that income level in the current year); or whose joint income including that person's spouse exceeded $300,000 in each of the two most recent years and who expects to reach that income level in the current year. Importantly, if securities are sold to any non-accredited investors, Rule 502(b) requires that the issuer provide each non-accredited investor with the information specified in that rule, simple to what is required by a prospectus.

Another potential exemption from registration is provided by Regulation S. Unlike Regulation D, however, *Regulation S does not provide an exemption from state securities registration.*

WHAT IS AN ISSUER?

Under Section 2(a) (4) of the Securities Act, an issuer is a person or entity who issues or proposes to issue any security. The enhanced informational requirements are an onerous requirement that the issuer can avoid by only selling to accredited investors. Rule 502(c) prohibits a general solicitation or advertising in the offer or sale of securities. Rule 502(d) proscribes the resale of securities sold under Regulation D unless the securities are registered or another exemption applies to the resale.

An exemption available for the resale of restricted securities is in Rule 144 promulgated under the Securities Act. Rule 144 states that securities held for at least six months are no longer restricted and may be resold without registration. It is the responsibility of the issuer to ensure that the purchasers of the securities do not violate the resale restrictions.

Rule 502(a) also states that offers and sales made within six months before and after the completion of a Regulation D offering might be considered as a part of that Regulation D offering or "integrated" into that offering. The SEC will look at the circumstances of all the offerings within this one-year integration window to determine whether separate sales are in fact part of the same offering.

The factors that the SEC looks at are whether: (I) the sales are part of a single plan of financing; (ii) the sales involve issuance of the same class of securities; (iii) the sales have been made at or about the same time; (iv) the same type of consideration is being received; and (v) the sales are made for the same general purpose.

Rule 503 requires an issuer offering securities in reliance on Regulation D to file a notice of sales with the SEC for each new offering of securities no later than 15 calendar days after the first sale of securities. To determine whether a separate Form D must be filed for a subsequent offering of the same type of securities, the issuer should evaluate the factors that the SEC uses to determine whether there is integration under Rule 502(a), such as whether the offering is part of a single plan of financing or made for the same general purpose.

The limitation on the manner of offering is one that most distinguishes a private placement offering from a public distribution.

To maintain the exemption under Regulation D as a private placement offering, issuers must pay careful attention not to engage in general solicitation or advertising.

WHAT IS A GENERAL SOLICITION?

If a direct investment vehicle or a regional center violates the prohibition on general solicitation and advertising under Rule 502(c), the Regulation D exemptions are no longer available and any securities sold under Regulation D will be voided. The regional center must register the
securities or find another available exemption.

General solicitation includes any advertisement, article, notice or other communication published in any newspaper, magazine, or similar media or broadcast over television or radio and any seminar or meeting whose attendees have been invited by the foregoing methods. This applies whether the general solicitation is conducted in the United States or abroad. Sending mass e-mails, newsletters or other mailings are considered general solicitations.

Activities by third party intermediaries such as immigration brokers or finders are included in the determination of whether a regional center or direct investment entity has complied with Rule 502(c). If an immigration attorney, for example, accepts fees from someone other than his or her own EB-5 investor-client the immigration attorney is acting as a third party intermediary and his activities will be evaluated within the context of Rule 502(c).

Both the EB-5 investor and the regional center should tread lightly with solicitation and marketing activities because the consequences of violating Rule 502(c) will be costly; to wit, any transaction in violation of Rule 502(c) will be voidable and the Regulation D exemption will no longer be available.

Neither an investor nor a regional center wants to be involved in an investment that will require registration; registration means extra time and extra money. Registration will enhance the need for disclosures; in fact, such registration would entail an initial public offering ("IPO"). To complete an IPO, the regional center would need at least three years of audited financials—or, if it qualifies as a "smaller reporting company," two years of comparative audited balance sheet data in annual financial statements.

The regional center or direct investment entity cannot offer or sell securities until the registration statement is effective. If the Regulation D exemption is no longer available, issuers will then have to find a separate exemption under each applicable state's securities laws.

Bottom line, EB-5 investors cannot afford to make investments associated with third party intermediaries engaging in general solicitation or advertising activities. It is the regional center's obligation (and the direct investment entity's obligation) to comply with the conditions under Regulation D. However, a potential investor is well advised to do his or her own due diligence to ensure that the regional center or direct investment entity is complying with all applicable securities laws.

The initial dissemination of information to potential investors with whom a regional center has no preexisting relationship may only be made in general terms and may not identify a specific investment opportunity. If there is a pre-existing relationship between the regional center nor direct investment entity and the potential investor, solicitation of the investor will not be considered general and references to specific investment opportunities can be made by the regional center or direct investment entity.

SEC no-action letters and releases posit that a pre-existing relationship can be formed through the use of a questionnaire to determine whether a potential investor is an accredited investor. The SEC has referred to the use of accredited investor questionnaires as essential to establishing a substantive pre-existing relationship.

One of the benefits of the Rule 506 exemption under Regulation D is that securities transactions pursuant to this regulation are exempt from any state securities registration requirements.

WHAT ARE COVERED SECURITIES?

In 1996, Congress passed The National Securities Markets Improvement Act ("NSMIA") preempting state securities laws when a transaction involves "covered securities." Securities exempt from registration under Rule 506 of Regulation D are among the transactions that are listed as "covered securities."

Under the NSMIA, however, states are still allowed to require notification of the exempt transaction and payment of a fee for such notification from the issuer. All states generally require that an issuer file a copy with it of the Form D filed with the SEC, along with a fee. In addition, the NSMIA does not preclude the states from requiring conditions other than registration of the securities, such as prohibiting issuers from paying remuneration to anyone who is not a registered broker-dealer or agent. The SEC has determined that a 30-day waiting period should exist between the determination of accredited investor status and the date an offering is made. This 30-day "safe harbor" provides regional centers and potential investors with a guideline.

Under Rule 503, an issuer selling securities in reliance on the exemptions provided for in Regulation D must file a Form D with the SEC. Federal rules also require broker-dealers to be registered.

Violation of the broker-dealer registration requirements may impose liability not only on the agent but also the regional center or direct investment entity. *The investment opportunity, if tainted, will also adversely affect the EB-5 investor.*

States generally prohibit issuers from paying anyone in consummating a securities transaction unless the recipient is a registered broker dealer or agent. All states require that broker-dealers and agents register in the states in which they operate. Performing due diligence, negotiating terms, soliciting investors and handling the funds of the investors are activities that states have determined qualify as broker-dealer activities. In addition, a third party who receives any transaction-based compensation in connection with a securities transaction will almost always Be deemed a broker-dealer.

On the other hand, if a third party does nothing more than provide the name and contact information of a potential investor to the issuer, the third party would be considered a "finder" rather than a broker-dealer.

The exception for finders is unclear in many instances because the concept of a finder is principally a construction of regulatory interpretations from various SEC no-action letters.

A potential EB-5 investor dealing with a third party intermediary may be unaware of the rules and regulations that apply to an intermediary's activities relating to a Regulation D offering. Recent SEC informal advisories warn that the use of unregistered broker-dealers will render the issuer liable as an aider and abettor of securities law violations under Section 20(e) of the Securities Exchange Act of 1934. As a result, a regional center or direct investment entity should be careful about payments to unregistered broker-dealers.

WHAT IS A BROKER-DEALER?

Generally, a broker-dealer is defined as any person who attempts to effectuate a securities transaction, and an agent is a person whose attempts to consummate a securities transaction on behalf of an issuer or broker-dealer.

Section 15 of the Securities Exchange Act of 1934, as amended, defines a "broker" as any person engaged in the business of effecting transactions in securities. Violation of this prohibition could affect the validity of an investment as a whole and therefore could potentially impact investors' ability to receive an EB-5 green card.

IN CONCLUSION

The EB-5 visa program, whether executed via the widely praised regional center pilot program or a direct investment regime, is unique, valuable and has a widely praised and successful history. It adds jobs and it gets the investor his or her, and their family, precious green cards. However, the investor should be award of additional safeguards provided by U.S. securities laws as well as the risks when working with a regional center or direct investment entity that chooses to ignore these laws.

Chapter Three: Direct Investments v. Regional Centers

Editor's Note: The following cursory list was compiled uncritically from two or three sources. The author is currently researching this topic and seeks feedback from readers. He is particularly looking for comments and suggestions that support the use of direct investments.

With direct investments the investor must:

1) Identify an investment project

2) submit a job creation study to the USCIS.

3) submit an economic impact study for the project to the USCIS

4) invest at least $1,000,000

5) assume direct management involvement in the project.

6) live in the area where the project is located with limited ability to return to his native country until he becomes a citizen (usually 5 years or more).

7) assume responsibility to create and document10 jobs

8) keep accurate records and file other reports on his business to the USCIS every 3 months.

9) create his own exit strategy.

Further, the investment must be in the form of equity, not debt, and the investor can only count direct new jobs created by his project for reporting to the USCIS; and the foreign investor and his family members are not eligible to be counted.

Projects for investment are limited in scope since pooled funds from several investors are not allowed and there is only one RB-5 investor in a project.

With Regional Centers:

1) A Regional Center must seek out and find investment projects that meet all of the requirements to qualify for the EB-5 visa program.

2) Investment through a Regional Center allows the EB-5 Client to invest only $500,000. A Regional Center can give the EB-5 Client investment options from which to choose.

3) MCFI requires a Private Placement Memorandum (PPM), a Subscription Agreement, a project management agreement and plan including the qualifications of the manager. The EB-5 Client can visit the project to meet the developers and manager before he invests.

4) Regional Centers manage investments for the foreign investor and the investor has no management responsibilities.

5) Regional Centers help the EB-5 Client comply with all of the

regulatory and reporting requirements of the USCIS, including the job creation and economic impact requirements,

6) In addition to direct job creation, Regional Centers are allowed to count indirect, imputed and construction jobs in their calculation of job creation for the EB-5 visa program...

7) Regional Centers can pool funds from several different investors allowing investment in much larger projects.

8) The EB-5 can live and work in any area of the U.S. He does not have to live in the area where the project is located...

9) Regional Centers can offer a wide variety of projects.

Part Two

Chapter Four: Business Brokers Acting as Broker-Dealers

The United States Supreme Court has held that the sale of a controlling interest in a business affected by the sale of its stock constitutes a securities transaction. Accordingly, the transaction is entitled to the protection of the federal securities laws. This chapter addresses broker-dealer registration requirements under the Exchange Act and the applicability of state blue sky laws to business brokers.

The recurring theme under federal and state law to determine if a business broker will be required to register as a broker-dealer or agent is whether he satisfies both the "engaged in business" and "effecting transactions" requirements of a securities broker-dealer or agent.

The "engaged in business" requirement implies either holding oneself out as available to perform or actually performing repeated securities transactions. Although the definition of broker does not share the "regular business" language with the definition of a dealer, it appears that more than isolated transactions are required before one must register as a securities broker.

In applying the "recurrence test," the SEC in its no-action letters has uniformly held that registration is not mandated under section 15(a)(1) of the Exchange Act if a person has never participated in securities transactions and does not anticipate making any further securities offerings.

The SEC staff has stated that section 15(a) of the Exchange Act requires registration of a person who has had prior experience as a securities salesman and might become involved in future offerings.

The regularity and frequency of turnover is a decisive factor in the broker-dealer status determination. For example, a person who had repeatedly sold interests in real estate ventures to investors as part of a real estate business was held to be a "dealer" and, therefore, was required to register.

It is apparent that a person may be required to register as a broker-dealer although a person's securities activities neither constitute his principal business or principal source of income. In addition, advertising by a person or entity may evidence being "engaged in business." Holding oneself out as available or interested in trading through general advertising can bring one within the "engaged in business" test.

Typically, there are five activities conducted by business brokers which may bring one within the definition of a broker-dealer or agent: (1) acting as a finder; (2) consulting independently with an issuer; (3) channeling customers to broker-dealers; (4) sharing in broker-dealer compensation; or (5) maintaining custody or possession of customers' funds or securities.

Generally, a finder brings together two entities interested in forming a business combination. The services of finders may vary from case to case. If a finder merely brings the parties together with no involvement in negotiating the price or any of the other terms of the transaction, he will not be acting as a broker. On the other hand, **a business broker acting as a finder will be deemed to be a broker if he participates in**

negotiations by advising on questions of value or performs other acts to facilitate the transaction.

The SEC staff has taken the position that individuals who do nothing more than bring merger or acquisition-minded persons or entities together and do not participate in negotiations or settlements probably are not brokers or dealers. On the other hand, persons who play an integral role in negotiating and effecting mergers or acquisitions that involve transactions in securities generally are deemed to be either a broker or dealer .

The SEC staff has addressed whether a business broker was required to register as a broker under section 15(a) of the Exchange Act.

The staff did not recommend enforcement action against the business broker even though the broker entered into listing agreements with businesses to sell the assets of these companies, advertised the assets of these companies, provided information supplied by the seller to prospective buyers, assisted in negotiations by transmitting documents between parties, and collected a commission based on the selling price. In taking this position the staff noted that a business broker need not register because: (1) he had a limited role in negotiations between the seller and buyer; (2) the businesses involved were going concerns; (3) only assets were advertised; (4) transactions effected by sales of securities would involve the sale of all the equity to one buyer or a group formed without the business broker's assistance; (5) no advice was rendered by the business broker as to whether to issue securities nor did it assess the value of securities sold; (6) the compensation did not vary according to whether the form of the transaction was an asset or stock sale; and (7) the business broker did not assist the buyers in obtaining financing, except that it could, at the parties' request, provide a list of potential lenders.

To avoid broker-dealer status, an independent consultant must not assist or supervise the sales efforts. The consultant must limit his activities to advising the issuer on how to develop the offering.

In *Church Of Christ v. National Plan, Inc.*, the court of appeals held that the evidence conclusively established that the defendant was a securities broker where the defendant: (1) assisted the issuer in doing all of the legal work concerning the offering; (2) completed all necessary printing; (3) handled all of the paper work in connection with the offering; (4) served as fiscal agent and trustee of the offering; (5) put on programs relating to the offering upon. The SEC staff held that a consultant retained to develop a proposed business plan of a new corporation, including the program for offering securities, need not register as a broker-dealer.

However the SEC staff concluded that registration would be required where a firm engaged in the following activities: (1) conducted a feasibility study to structure the issuance of securities; (2) prepared an outline for the issuer with recommendations relating to the issue; (3) searched out and obtained a registered broker-dealer to act as managing underwriter; (4) prepared the registration statement and handled its processing; (5) assisted broker-dealers and their representatives in analyzing and developing marketing techniques with respect to the offering; (6) provided training programs for representatives of the broker-dealers upon request; and (7) received a commission based on the size of the offering.

In determining whether a person is a broker-dealer, the SEC staff has also examined whether the compensation is fixed as opposed to being transaction-based. The SEC has concluded that attorneys, accountants, insurance brokers, and financial service organizations "who for a fee assist promoters or other issuers in the sale of securities" are considered to be brokers if they have been "retained by an issuer specifically for the purpose of selling securities to the public and generally receive transaction-based compensation." However, the SEC staff held that registration was not required where a company received negotiated fees relating to "the overall size of the financing that the client wished to arrange, which generally would not be payable unless the financing clods successfully."

The conduct of a business broker may bring him within the definition of an "underwriter" if his services result in "participation in the undertaking rather than that of a mere interest in it."

Section 2(11) of the Securities Act of 1933 defines underwriter to include "any person who ... offers or sells for an issuer in connection with the distribution of any security, or participates or has a direct or indirect participation in any such undertaking .... Thus, a business broker may be deemed an underwriter if his services include effecting a public distribution of securities or the solicitation of indications of interest to purchase securities.

In a 1974 no-action letter, the SEC took a no-action position on a finder whose activities included introducing parties to negotiate acquisitions of businesses or assets. The finder did not become involved in the negotiations of parties or evaluation of the proposed transaction. However, the SEC indicated that if the finder's business included solicitation of investors' indications of interest in a security, the finder would be deemed an underwriter as defined in section 2(11) of the Securities Act.

The sale of a security by a unregistered broker-dealer or agent may result in both civil and criminal liability for the broker-dealer or agent and the issuer or seller.

The civil remedies available to a purchaser of securities from an unlicensed broker-dealer may be classified into three categories: remedies at common law; express or implied remedies under federal law; and express or implied remedies under state blue sky laws. In addition to the civil remedies, the Securities and Exchange Commission as well as the Commissioner of Securities for the relevant state is empowered to obtain injunctions against unregistered persons engaging in securities brokerage activity. Moreover, the Securities and Exchange Commission and the state Commissioner of Securities

The courts are divided about whether there is an implied right of recovery under the Exchange Act for buyers or sellers of securities when a broker or dealer fails to register under section 15(a) of the Act. Section 15(a), by its terms, does not mandate express liability for its violation.

Hence, courts have generally held that there is no private right of action for violations of section 15 of the Exchange Act.

If the commissioner has reason to believe that any security is being or has been offered or sold in this state by any unlicensed person in violation of this chapter or any rule or order hereunder, the commissioner may by order summarily prohibit such person from further offers or sales of securities in this state until licensed.

"It shall be unlawful for any broker or dealer which is either a person other than a natural person or a natural person not associated with a broker or dealer which is a person other than a natural person (other than such a broker or dealer whose business is exclusively intrastate and who does not make use of any facility of a national securities exchange) to make use of the mails or any means or instrumentality of interstate commerce to effect any transactions in, or to induce or attempt to induce the purchase or sale of, any security (other than an exempted security or commercial paper, bankers' acceptances, or commercial bills) unless such broker or dealer is registered in accordance with subsection (b) of this section." 15 U.S.C. § 78a (l). By contrast, courts have held that a private cause of action can be founded upon section 29(b) of the Act. Section 29(b) provides: [e]very contract made in violation of any provision of [the Act] ... and every contract ... the performance of which involves the violation of ... any provision of [the Act] ...shall be void ... as regards the rights of any person who, in violation of any such provision ... shall have made or engaged in the performance of any such contract."

Section 29(b) of the Exchange Act permits a party to a contract to seek rescission if he can show that "(1) the contract involved a 'prohibited transaction' [under the Exchange Act], (2) he is in contractual private with the defendant, and (3) he is 'in the class of persons the Act was designed to protect.' Notwithstanding the courts' refusal to imply a private cause of action under section 15(a), courts have held that section 29(b) creates an implied private cause of action for rescission or similar equitable relief 135 Consequently, a section 29(b) claim can be based on an Exchange Act provision that does not contain private rights of action but the ordinary equitable defenses of estoppel, waiver, and laches are applicable. *In Regional Properties, Inc. v. Financial & Real Estate Consulting Co.,*

In determining whether injunctive relief is warranted under the federal securities laws, courts have examined whether "there is a reasonable likelihood of further violation in the future."

Addressing this issue in the context of a broker-dealer's failure to register, a district court examined the following factors: (1) the likelihood of future violations; (2) the degree of scienter involved; (3) the sincerity of defendant's assurances against future violations; (4) the isolated or recurrent nature of the infraction; (5) defendant's recognition of the wrongful nature of his conduct; and (6) the likelihood, because of defendant's professional occupation, that future violations might occur.1

Given the unregistered broker's history of securities law violations, the court granted a permanent injunction.

Although the degree of scienter may be a factor as to whether an injunction should be issued, it has been held in a case involving a claim for injunctive relief, that section 15(a)(1) contains no language from which a scienter requirement may be derived.

Courts have also enjoined a person from advertising when such conduct would cause the person to qualify as a broker-dealer. For example, a person who advertised in a newspaper with interstate circulation that he could save customers seventy percent on their brokerage commissions and that no commissions would be charged if the customer maintained a $500 balance in his account was enjoined for not registering as a broker-dealer.'

Section 15(b) (4) of the Exchange Act sets forth the Commission's authority to institute disciplinary proceedings against broker-dealers.

Under this section the Commission may order any of the following for a willful failure to register: (1) censure; (2) limitations on activities, functions or operations; (3) suspension of registration for a period not to exceed twelve months; and (4) revocation of registration. In addition, the Commission may order any of the above if one is permanently or temporarily enjoined from acting as a

As previously noted, a purchaser of securities may seek rescission under section 29(b) of the Exchange Act. Thus, a rescission action under section 29(b) based upon a section15(a) violation will have a greater impact on a seller or an issuer than the broker-dealer if it results in the business sale being voided. Although a purchaser of securities can obtain equitable relief against an issuer or seller, it is doubtful that money damages can be obtained.

Moreover, given the absence of an implied right of action under section15(a), it is unlikely that a purchaser of securities could rely on section 20(a) of the Exchange Act to impose liability on a seller of a business. Section 20(a) provides that a controlling person may be jointly and severally liable with the controlled person for securities violations under certain circumstances.

However, the common law action of respondent superior may be available to a purchaser of securities against a seller or issuer if an unlicensed broker-dealer was engaged to sell a business. The client needs to minimize the scope of activities in connection with the sale of a business. This may be accomplished by merely introducing the parties and not engaging in substantive business

If the business broker has passed the required NASD exams, he may be licensed in the state as an agent of the issuer and receive commissions without jeopardizing the applicable transactional exemption. In addition to the federal and state registration requirements, a broker-dealer is required to become a member of the appropriate self-regulating organization, such as the National Association of Securities (NASD). Broker-dealers that affiliate with the NASD are subject to NASD reporting and examination requirements.

The legislative history of the Exchange Act and state blue sky laws indicate an intent to regulate the competence and character of those effecting securities transactions. However, the characterization of those who engage in controlling interest business sales as securities brokers creates untoward results, in that, *a purchaser of a business who is able to pursue a claim against a business broker for failure to register will also benefit by the strict liability imposed upon the seller or issuer of the business. Consequently, the purchaser of the business has effectively been granted a "put" in the stock of the company during the civil statute of limitations.*

Chapter Five: Brokers, Dealers and Finders

Raising capital for EB-5 projects can be difficult. Depending upon how they introduce investors, business brokers and others may be required to register as "broker-dealers." If they fail to register, a regional center or direct investment promoter using unregistered broker-dealers may face significant securities law challenges.

Broker-dealers are regulated under the Securities Exchange Act of 1934 (the "Exchange Act"). Many states also regulate broker-dealers through their "blue sky laws." For example, California law provides a right of rescission, recovery of additional damages, and an extended statute of limitations for investors against an unlicensed broker-dealer. "Brokers" and "dealers" must register with the Securities Exchange Commission using Form BD and join a self-regulatory organization and, in most cases, the Securities Investor Protection Corporation.

The Exchange Act makes it unlawful for any broker or dealer to "effect any transactions in, or to induce or attempt to induce the purchase or sale of, any security" unless that broker or dealer is registered with the SEC. Both regional centers and direct investment entities must recognize the need of persons helping raise capital on their behalf to register as brokers.

A business broker or other finder who refers a potential investor to a regional center or direct investment and receives in a commission is likely acting as a broker. Failure to register could result in serious adverse consequences to an unregistered broker-dealer, including injunctive or disciplinary action against the person as well as and exposure to investor suits, fines, and penalties, and even criminal prosecution. The consequences against a regional center or direct investment entity are similarly grave, including investor suits and possibly criminal prosecution.

The Exchange Act defines a "broker" as "any person engaged in the business of effecting transactions in securities for the account of others," and a "dealer" as "any person engaged in the business of buying and selling securities for his own account, through a broker or otherwise". A broker sells securities for clients, while a dealer sells securities for itself. In determining whether a person or a company is a broker or a dealer, the SEC looks at the activities in which the person or business engages.

The SEC looks at "activities," and not just one "activity." The SEC provides the following as general guidance as to whether a person or company is a broker or dealer. Answering "yes" to any of the questions may indicate the need to register as a broker or dealer:

Broker

1. Do you participate in important parts of a securities transaction, including solicitation, negotiation, or execution of the transaction?

2. Does your compensation for participation in the transaction depend upon, or is it related to, the outcome or size of the transaction or deal? Do you receive trailing commissions, such as 12b1 fees? Do you receive any other transaction-related compensation?

3. Are you otherwise engaged in the business of effecting

or facilitating securities transactions?

4. Do you handle the securities or funds of others in connection with securities transactions?

Dealer

1. Do you advertise or otherwise let others know that you are in the business of buying and selling securities?

2. Do you do business with the public (either retail or institutional)?

3. Do you make a market in, or quote prices for both purchases and sales of, one or more securities?

4. Do you participate in a "selling group" or otherwise underwrite securities?

5. Do you provide services to investors, such as handling money and securities, extending credit, or giving investment advice?

6. Do you write derivatives contracts that are securities?

Finder

Many believe that a person can avoid classification as a broker by claiming to be a "finder." It is true that regional centers and direct investment entities may freely use finders. However, labeling oneself a finder is not dispositive. If one is engaged in the activities of a broker-dealer, registration is still required. In many cases, people who claim to be finders actually are brokers and must register under the Exchange Act.

A true finder introduces an investor in exchange for a fee that is paid regardless of whether the investor ultimately invests or not. A true finder does not solicit investors or negotiate, recommend, provide advice or information.

Regional centers and direct investment entities using finders must ensure that the finder is a legitimate finder. In engagement letters with finders, regional centers and direct investment entities should include indemnification clauses for any liability incurred as a result of the finder's failure to register as a broker-dealer. Providing covenants that clearly spell out prohibited activities may be helpful both in educating unsophisticated finders about the broker-dealer laws, as well as affording the regional center or direct investment entity with a breach of contract claim.

All broker-dealers are finders, but not all finders are broker-dealers. Finders do not need to be registered but broker-dealers do. If a person does anything other than provide an introduction of a potential investor, or takes compensation that is dependent on the whether the investment is made, that person is a broker-dealer and must be registered.

Chapter Six: Purchaser Representatives

Any EB-5 regional center promoter or direct investment developer must comply with the regulations from USCIS under the immigration law, as well as be aware of information disclosure, maximum investment amount, maximum number of non-accredited investors allowed, and related investment requirements under the Securities Exchange Commission regulations.

To qualify as a private placement, an offering must meet either the requirement of Sections 3(b) or 4(2) of the 1933 Act or must follow the conditions set out under Regulation D of the 1933 Act. Those claiming exemption from the 1933 Act carry the burden of proving that the activities come within that exemption.

Up to 35 non-accredited investors are allowed under sections 505 and 506 of Regulation D of the Securities Act; no limits are put on any number of investors

An investor who meets the net worth requirements for an accredited investor under the Securities & Exchange Commission's Regulation D is an accredited investor—this is someone who has a net worth of at least $1 million (including spouse) and who earned more than $200,000 annually ($300,000 with spouse) in the last two years.

When a company raises private equity for project, it is able to receive unlimited investments from accredited investors, while only 35 non-accredited investors are allowed to invest. However, the maximum number of non-accredited investors allowed in a private placement is unlimited if exempt under Rule 504, up to 35 if exempt under rule 505, or up to 35 *sophisticated investors* if exempt under Rule 506.

Security law has different information disclosure requirements for accredited investors and for non-accredited investors. Under the exemptions allowed by SEC Regulation D, the maximum investment amount for an EB-5 visa is $1 million, $5 million, or unlimited – depending on which exemption is claimed.

Under the exemptions allowed by current federal statutes and SEC regulations, the maximum investment amount allowed in a private placement is $1 million if exempt under Rule 504, $5 million if exempt under rule 505, or unlimited if exempt under Rule 506. Section 4(2) of the Federal Securities Act exempts from registration "transactions by an issuer not involving any public offering." It was under this mandate from Congress that the SEC promulgated rules to specify what private placements qualify as not involving any public offering.

Rule 504 provides an exemption for the offer and sale of up to $1,000,000 of securities in a 12-month period. No public solicitation or advertising of the securities is allowed. Purchasers receive "restricted" securities, meaning that they may not sell the securities without registration or an applicable exemption. Note that there is no maximum number of accredited or non-accredited investors for this exemption to apply.

Rule 505 provides an exemption for offers and sales of securities totaling up to $5 million in any 12-month period. Under this exemption, you may sell to an unlimited number of "accredited investors" and up to 35 other persons who do not need to satisfy the sophistication or wealth standards associated with other exemptions.

Rule 506 is a "safe harbor" for the private offering exemption. You can raise an unlimited amount of capital; there is no maximum amount for this exemption. Accordingly, the exemption available in this section is the only one available for any investment projects where the capital raised exceeds $5 million. You can sell securities to an unlimited number of accredited investors and up to 35 other purchasers. These purchasers must be sophisticated, or they must rely upon sophisticated purchaser representatives.

Unlike Rule 505, all non-accredited investors, either alone or with a purchaser representative, must be sophisticated - that is, they must have sufficient knowledge and experience in financial and business matters to make them capable of evaluating the merits and risks of the prospective investment.

Financial statement requirements are the same as for Rule 505; and purchasers receive "restricted" securities. Consequently, purchasers may not freely trade the securities in the secondary market after the offering.

EB-5 Regional Centers and direct investment promoters may want to consider a "Purchaser Representative." If it is determined that a particular purchaser is not sufficiently sophisticated in business matters to effectively evaluate the investment opportunity, then he or she must be assisted by a "purchaser representative," i.e., a person possessing the requisite sophistication (chosen by the purchaser) who is able to and does assist in evaluating the investment opportunity and who is not an affiliate of the issuer, not the brokerage firm.

In order to qualify for the exemption under Rule 506, the Purchaser Representative must have knowledge and experience in financial and business matter; must disclose in writing any prior relationship between the Purchaser Representative and the Issuer; and is acknowledged by the purchaser in writing to be his or her Purchaser Representative.

Rule 501 of Regulation D of the Securities Act of 1993 reads as follows:

"Purchaser representative shall mean any person who satisfies all of the following conditions or who the issuer reasonably believes satisfies all of the following conditions:

1. Is not an affiliate, director, officer or other employee of the issuer, or beneficial owner of 10 percent or more of any class of the equity securities or10 percent or more of the equity interest in the issuer, except where the purchaser is?

- A relative of the purchaser representative by blood, marriage or adoption and not more remote than a first cousin;
- A trust or estate in which the purchaser representative and any persons related to him as specified in paragraph (h)(1)(I) or (h)1(iii) of this section collectively have more than 50 percent of the beneficial interest (excluding contingent interest) or of which the purchaser representative serves as trustee, executor, or in any similar capacity; or
- A corporation or other organization of which the purchaser representative and any persons related to him as specified in paragraph (h)(1)(I) or (h)(1)(ii) of this

section collectively are the beneficial owners of more than 50 percent of the equity securities (excluding directors' qualifying shares) or equity interests;

2. Has such knowledge and experience in financial and business matters that he is capable of evaluating, alone, or together with other purchaser representatives of the purchaser, or together with the purchaser, the merits and risks of the prospective investment;

3. Is acknowledged by the purchaser in writing, during the course of the transaction, to be his purchaser representative in connection with evaluating the merits and risks of the prospective investment;

4. Discloses to the purchaser in writing a reasonable time prior

5. to the sale of securities to that purchaser any material relationship between himself or

his affiliates and the issuer or its affiliates that then exists, that is mutually

understood to be contemplated, or that has existed at any time during

the previous two years, and any compensation received or to be received

as a result of such relationship."

Part Three

Chapter Seven: EB-5 Law and Practice Following the JOBS Act

The SEC's proposed rules under the JOBS Act will change the practice of law relating to EB-5 offerings. Regional centers and other EB-5 issuers ("direct investments") will have more latitude with respect to general solicitations and general advertisements. However, the effort and cost to comply with securities law will increase significantly due to the "reasonable steps" requirement. Proof of "reasonable steps" taken to verify accredited investor status will now be a condition to the availability of the exemption under Rule 506 (c). Lawyers working in this field will need some familiarity with both securities law and EB-5 law.

The most commonly used exemption in EB-5 offerings is Regulation D (private placements). Regulation S offshore offerings exemptions are far less frequently used. Without either exemption, issuers must register their offerings with the SEC and disclose information similar to what public offerings require. Failure to comply subjects an issuer to prohibitive penalties and fines and entitles EB-5 investors to recover their full investment.

The SEC's proposed rules will repeal the prohibition against general solicitation and general advertising rules for private placement offerings conducted pursuant to Rule 506 of Regulation D, *provided*:

- all purchasers are accredited investors;
- issuers take reasonable steps to verify that the purchasers are accredited investors; and
- Issuers indicate on the Form D filing that there has been general solicitation and/or general advertising.

EB-5 issuers will now be able to advertise via website advertisements, newspapers, radio, internet broadcasts and e-mail.

Most issuers of EB-5 securities rely on a suitability questionnaire to establish whether an investor qualifies as an accredited investor. The SEC has allowed issuers to rely on these representations as long as the issuer has no reason to believe that the representation is incorrect. Now, however, the EB-5 issuer will be required to take "reasonable steps" to *verify* that the purchasers are accredited investors. It will not be good enough that a purchaser merely clams his is an accredited investor; the issuers must take "reasonable steps" to establish that the investor is in fact an accredited investor.

The SEC has made it clear that the tried and true "questionnaire practice" will no longer be sufficient. The SEC has provided examples of factors it will consider under the new rules:

- the type of accredited investor that the investor claims to be;
- the type of information the issuer has about the investor;
- the manner in which the investor was solicited to participate in the offering; and
- the terms of the offering such as the minimum investment amount.

The amount and type of information the issuer possesses about a purchaser will be a major factor in determining what other steps may be appropriate. For instance, an issuer that solicits new investors through a website accessible to the general public or through a widely disseminated email or social media solicitation will be obligated to take greater measures to verify accredited investor status than an issuer that solicits new investors from a database of pre-screened accredited investors maintained by a reliable third party, such as a registered broker-dealer.

EB-5 offerings will always be made to natural persons. They are most commonly done with a website or via email as a result of the practical challenge of soliciting purchasers outside of the U.S. Based on the proposed rules issuers will have to take more steps than before to verify the accredited investor status of investors sought via these public forums.

EB-5 issuers may want to ask for source of funds documents from prospective investors earlier rather than later—even before providing investors with a Private Placement Memorandum or Subscription Agreement. Further, EB-5 issuers will still have to consider whether the source of funds documentation is sufficient to meet the burden of the proposed "reasonable steps" requirement. For example, if an investor's source of funds is a gift, source of funds documentation will be less useful in verifying accredited investor status than if the source of funds was occasioned by a usual course of business transaction.

The SEC proposed rules stipulate that the agency will take into account whether the investment was made with cash "financed by any third party." Conversely, if there is a high minimum amount of investment, the SEC states it may be reasonable for an issuer to take *fewer* steps to verify accredited investor status. As always, if a purchaser provides false or fraudulent information or documentation, an EB-5 issuer will not face liability provided it did not reasonably know that the information was false or fraudulent.

Any EB-5 issuer that relies on an exemption from registration pursuant to Regulation D is required to file a Form D (Notice of Exempt Offering of Securities with the SEC) within 15 days after the first sale of securities in the offering.

The Form D discloses:

- information regarding the issuer of the securities;
- information about related persons (executive officers, directors, and promoters);
- identification of the exemption or exemptions being claimed for the offering;
- factual information about the offering, such as the duration of the offering, the type of securities offered, and any commissions or other payments to third parties in connection with the offering on behalf of the issuer.

The SEC's proposed new rules will amend the Form D to add a new check box for an issuer to indicate that it is relying on the new "Rule 506 (c)" exemption allowing general solicitation. *The SEC's view is that this disclosure will allow it to better monitor private offerings conducted using general solicitation and that purchasers in those transactions need more oversight and protection against fraudulent activities by issuers.*

Many EB-5 issuers rely on the dual protections afforded by the Regulation D and Regulation S exemptions. Dual exemptions are an effective way to reduce securities law risk, especially since the SEC has not given much guidance with respect to certain EB-5 practices.

The Regulation S "offshore exemption" has several requirements, one of which is that there should be no "directed selling efforts" within the United States. Any methods of general solicitation or general advertisement such as online advertisement (which can include posting descriptions of an offering on an EB-5 issuer's website) may be deemed to be directed sales efforts. *Insofar as these selling efforts are accessible to individuals in the United States, a regional center or other EB-5 issuer utilizing these advertisements would not be in compliance with Regulation S. Therefore, taking advantage of the freedom to conduct a general solicitation or general advertisement under the proposed rules relating to Regulation D may eliminate a regional center's or other EB-5 issuer's ability to rely on Regulation S.*

If an EB-5 issuer conducts a general solicitation or general advertisement under the proposed rules, but does not take reasonable steps to verify the accredited investor status of proposed investors, the issuer is in danger of having no valid exemption to the registration requirement.

Regional centers and other EB-5 issuers must take significant measures to adopt policies and procedures governing how they obtain and maintain documentation regarding potential purchasers' financial information and accredited investor status. Importantly, any issuer wishing to take advantage of the new general solicitation and general advertisement rules will be required to alert the SEC of that fact on a Form D, filed shortly after the offering commences.

In conclusion, any marketing advantages sought from general solicitation and general advertisements must be weighed against the potential pitfalls of losing a securities law exemption. Accordingly, some EB-5 issuers will not be best served by taking advantage of the greater marketing opportunities allowed by the new rules.

Chapter 8: Implementing the JOBS Act with Changes to Rule 506

The Dodd-Frank Act has profound implications that will touch financial services and other industries. The SEC issued a proposal for the new Rule 506(c) under the Securities Act, which would implement the mandate of the JOBS Act to allow for the use of general solicitation and advertising in private offerings where the only purchasers are accredited investors. Since the proposal's release, the SEC has been receiving comment letters from state securities regulators, individuals, and trade groups.

A selective overview of some regulators' comments follows:

From NASAA:

1. "Fraudulent Rule 506 offerings were ranked as 'the most common product or scheme leading to enforcement actions by state securities regulators.'"
2. "State securities regulators are the primary enforcers of anti-fraud provisions; in regard to Rule 506 offerings the SEC initiated 124 total 'securities offerings' enforcement actions while state regulators took more than 200 enforcement actions relating to Rule 506 offerings."
3. "**The Commission has never brought a single action against a company for violating Rule 503 for failing to file Form D** [bold editors], and we are unaware of any subsequent enforcement actions to enforce the filing requirements. However, state regulators routinely

review Form D to ensure that the offerings actually qualify for an exemption under Rule 506 and to look for "red flags" that may indicate a fraudulent offering."

4. "Form D filings should be required prior to public advertising in order to put state securities regulators on notice that a general solicitation offering will be taking the SEC issued a proposal for new Rule 506(c) under the Securities Act, which would implement the mandate of the JOBS Act to allow for the use of general solicitation and advertising in private offerings where the only purchasers are accredited investors. Since the proposal's release, the SEC has been receiving comment letters from state securities regulators, individuals, and trade groups (otherwise a state regulator who sees a public advertisement will have no way of knowing if it is part of a Rule 506 compliant offering or is a part of an unregistered offering, non-exempt public offering)."

5. **"Even though the JOBS Act directed the SEC to 'require the issuer to take reasonable steps to verify that purchasers of the securities are accredited investors, using such methods as are determined by the Commission,' the SEC has utterly failed to fulfill the second part of this mandate – determining appropriate methods**. [bold editors]. Since the SEC has only parroted the "reasonable steps" language from the JOBS Act, state regulators will be stuck making case by case judgment calls, resulting in

inconsistent interpretations, state to state, and in increased litigation."
6. "The SEC should adopt non-exclusive safe harbors for verification of accredited investor status in order to provide regulators and market participants with some certainty. The NASAA provides several proposals for safe harbors, including reliance on broker-dealers for verification."
7. **"NASAA is dismayed by the SEC's willingness to implement the provisions of the JOBS Act allowing the use of general solicitation without also fulfilling the requirement of the JOBS Act that the SEC adopt rules to disqualify bad actors from using general solicitation in private offerings."** [bold editors]
8. "The SEC should place reasonable restrictions on the content of the advertising that can be used, similar to the restrictions described in CF Disclosure Guidance: Topic No. 3 (released in December 2011) – for example, requiring a balanced presentation of risks and rewards of the potential investment, and requiring that any statements contained in the advertising be consistent with offering documents. One concern is that 'puffing' type claims that are permissible in the advertising world generally could result in securities law liability for unwary issuers. With respect to private funds, there should be a separate set of rules comparable to restrictions that apply to mutual funds, similar in content to Rule 482, the standard from Rule 156, and Rule

206-4(8).

From AFL-CIO / AFR:

1. "The SEC should update the accredited investor definition as a basic safeguard, and should consider restricting Rule 506 offerings that use general solicitation to a new defined subset of accredited investors, called 'Large Accredited Investors' that would satisfy higher threshold amounts, such as a net worth of $2.5 million or income of at least $400,000."

2. "The SEC should prohibit private funds relying on the exemptions in Sections 3(c) (1) and (7) of the Investment Company Act – the entities that use Rule 506 offerings the most often – from using general solicitation, because the congressional intent for the lift of the ban on general solicitation was clearly aimed at small businesses rather than hedge funds and private equity funds."

3. "The SEC should require that any advertising materials an issue intends to use in connection with an offering be pre-filed with the SEC (similar to FINRA's requirement that broker-dealers pre-file similar materials) and create and/or enhance record keeping requirements with respect to matters such as investor qualifications and advertisements actually used in the offering."

From Consumer Federation of America:

1. "The SEC has unnecessarily restricted the scope of its proposed rule and its request for comments: **Unaccountably, the Commission only requests comment on its proposed approach to verification of accredited investor status and its proposed addition of a**

checkbox to Form D, dismissing without justification other issues and alternative regulatory approaches that have been brought to its attention." [bold editors]
2. "The SEC already fails to devote sufficient resources to oversight of Rule 506 offerings, and has repeatedly failed to take action in the face of rule violations, as noted in a 2009 Inspector General's report. The "reasonable steps" standard proposed by the SEC will be difficult to enforce and will further overwhelm the SEC's enforcement resources."
3. "If an issuer relies on a third party to verify that an investor is an accredited investor, the third party should be under obligations to maintain the accuracy of its information and safeguard investor data, at a minimum."
4. "The accredited investor definition should be broadened to require financial sophistication, not just a relatively high income or net worth, which are not reliable indicators of investment experience and have not been appropriately adjusted in the three decades since they were originally proposed."

From AILA:

"Unfortunately, as currently administered by USCIS, the EB-5 program is not realizing its full potential. Investment and job-creating are being thwarted by ever longer USCIS processing delays and rules that change in the middle of the process with no notice. This has created unpredictability and rising denial rates. This is having a chilling effect on foreign investors."

1. **Currently, 60% to 65% of the regional center applications are denied.** This is an indication that the program is clearly not functioning as it

should, and the 35% to 40% that *are* approved are frequently approved either too late to enable the project to go forward. Moreover, the frequency of requests for additional evidence ("RFE's")—too often several successive requests—shows that USCIS is less than clear with stakeholders with respect to what it is seeking.

2. AILA's EB-5 Committee has spent a great deal of time studying the problems that are endemic to the EB-5 program. The Committee suggests that the following "10 Point Program" could be implemented rather easily and could ultimately save the EB-5 program and maximize its job-creating potential:

    a) Provide a forum where every 90 days USCIS representatives advise regional center stakeholders of the issues it is seeing in applications that are producing the largest number of denials. At the same forum, allow regional center stakeholders to provide lists of issues on which there is a lack of clarity.

    b) b) When new standards are going to be implemented that will affect large numbers of applications (whether it involves the methodology for the counting of jobs that will be created, or the structure of bridge financing, or any other aspect of an EB-5 transaction), provide notice to stakeholders in advance rather than issuing large numbers of RFEs on issues that were not issues at the time of filing.

    c) Implement USCIS Director Mayorkas' idea of a Decision Board as promptly as possible. This Decision Board would be made up of economists and business analysts and would meet or conference with regional center applicants to discuss any issues that need to be resolved before a project can be approved.

d) Hire a sufficient number of examiners to bring processing times to levels that make some sense in a time-sensitive, job-creating program such as EB-5.

e) Instruct examiners that, except in rare instances, multiple RFEs should not be issued.

f) Publish meaningful guidelines on what adjudicators want to see when adjudicating a regional center application. Most denials and RFEs are based on often-changing policies that are not contained in any regulation or even any government-issued memorandum

g) Make the regional center amendment process workable. Regional Centers are approved for specific geographical areas, specific industry codes and specific economic methodologies for counting job creation. Right now, if a regional center wants to amend its geography, economic methodology or industry code, the published processing time is 8 months – longer than filing a new regional center application. This is unworkable.

USCIS has created a process – the exemplar I-526 – that enables a regional center to have a project approved for EB-5 investment prior to receiving investments. **The problem is that, despite a $6,230 fee and an 8 month processing time, USCIS does not consider itself bound by any approval**. USCIS must make this process meaningful as a way of saving time and adjudicatory resources. If it is not meaningful, stakeholders should not be expected to pay large filing fees and wait long periods of time; and the process should be eliminated...

Developers who invest hundreds of thousands of dollars putting together projects to present to USCIS deserve clarity and consistency. These prescriptions could be implemented immediately. The result would be not only a benefit to developers but also to the country, which would attract greater amounts of foreign direct investment and create more jobs for U.S. workers. We hope that USCIS will look favorably upon these constructive suggestions.

Part Four

Chapter 9: The Regulation S Safe Harbor

Regulation S is a safe harbor for offers and sales that occur outside the United States; it permits transactions that are not subject to the registration obligations imposed by Section 5.

Regulation S provides safe harbor exemptions for specified transactions. The offer or sale must occur in an "offshore transaction"—meaning the buyer is offshore at the time of the offer or sale. Further, the transaction must not include a pre-arranged U.S. buyer. And, of course, there must be not selling efforts made in the United States by the issuer, a distributor, any of their respective affiliates, or any person acting on behalf of any of the.

Rule 903 provides specific rules for offerings by issuers, distributors and their respective affiliates.

(a) securities of a "foreign issuer" for which there is no "substantial U.S. market interest (as defined below), (b) securities offered by a "foreign issuer" in "overseas directed offerings" (as defined below, (c) non-convertible debt securities of a domestic issuer offered in overseas directed offerings that are denominated in a currency other than U.S. dollars, and (d) securities backed by the full faith and credit of a foreign government.

An example of the restrictions that apply to Category 1 equity offerings is attached as Exhibit A. In these cases, only the general conditions referred to above must be observed.

Category 2:

(a) equity offerings by reporting foreign issuers, and (b) offerings of debt securities and non-convertible, non-participating preferred <u>stock</u> by reporting issuers or non-reporting foreign issuers. To be treated as a qualified reporting issuer, the issuer must have filed all required reports for at least twelve months prior to the offer or sale, or such shorter period during which the issuer was subject to the reporting obligation.

Offering Restrictions must be observed, which include prohibitions on resales to U.S. Persons during the distribution compliance period, in addition to the application of the general conditions. Generally, a 40day distribution compliance period (i.e., the period during which the restrictions required by the particular category remain in effect) will apply, which will have to be codified in a written agreement with each distributor and reflected in the offering documentation and on all confirmations issued to distributors and others receiving transaction-based compensation and to purchasers during the distribution compliance period.

(A safe harbor exemption is an exemption that is not the exclusive means that must be employed to fall within a more general exemption or jurisdictional limitation. By promulgating a safe harbor, the SEC is affirming that someone complying with its requirements will definitely have the benefit of the broader exemption or limitation.)

Category 3:

Offerings of all other securities, including (a) equity offerings by domestic reporting issuers, (b) offerings of equity securities by non-reporting foreign issuers for which there is a substantial U.S. market interest and (c) offerings by U.S. issuers that are not reporting issuers. These offerings are subject to the most stringent conditions.

> For debt securities the offering restrictions are the same as for Category 2, plus the need to use a temporary global certificate to support the 40-day distribution compliance period.
> For equity securities, the distribution compliance period is increased to one year, and the purchaser must also provide a certification as to its non-U.S. status and must agree not to resell to a U.S. Person except in accordance with U.S. requirements, in addition to compliance with the restrictions applicable to Category 2

> The securities of a domestic issuer must bear a restrictive legend, supported by stop transfer instructions.

The documentation required in the case of such issuers must refer to the prohibition on certain hedging transactions during the distribution compliance period that would have the effect of pre-selling, the securities into the United States and distributors must agree in writing to observe this prohibition. Rule 904 provides a safe harbor for certain resale transactions by persons other than the issuer, a distributor, any of their respective affiliates (except any officer or director who is an affiliate solely by virtue of such office), or any person acting on their behalf. They are subject to the following conditions:

1. All permitted sellers are subject to the general conditions.
2. In the case of a seller who is a dealer or a person receiving any remuneration, a resale cannot be

knowingly made to a U.S. Person prior to the end of the relevant distribution compliance period. A confirmation stating the applicable securities law restrictions must be sent to any other dealer or person receiving selling compensation   person.
3. No special compensation can be paid if the seller is an officer   or   director   of   the   issuer.
4. The safe harbor is not available to "affiliates" of the issuer, except where affiliation arises solely from the status of the seller as an officer or director. An "affiliate" is any person controlling, controlled by or under common control with the issuer. "Control" for this purpose means de facto control. A strong inference of control based upon voting influence often arises at the 10% threshold, although other factors may demonstrate or   point   away   from   control.
5. Transactions must be effected through a "designated offshore securities market" in a transaction not pre-arranged with a U.S. Person or in a transaction involving a buyer outside of the United States at the time the buy order   is   originated.
6. Care must be taken to ensure that the transaction does not involve a scheme to evade the Securities Act registration requirements, including for the purpose of washing off transfer restrictions.

Rule 905 provides that equity securities of domestic issuers acquired from the issuer, distributor, or any of their respective affiliates in a transaction subject to the safe harbor rules discussed above are deemed to be restricted securities, and resales by any offshore purchaser must be made pursuant to Regulation S or another exemption from Securities Act registration.

The   following   definitions   are   integral   to   an understanding of Regulation S.

1. "U.S. Person": For individuals, based largely on residence, rather than nationality.
2. Entities have residence largely based upon where they are formed, with the exception of identifiable branches of entities, which may themselves be treated as the equivalent of separate organizations. Accredited investors can form an offshore entity that will be treated as a non-U.S. Person for this purpose.
3. Detailed rules govern trusts and estates, and other professional fiduciaries, which are designed to mitigate disadvantages to U.S. professional fiduciaries by ensuing that, subject to certain conditions, offers to them for the account of non-U.S. Persons will not trigger Securities Act registration, despite the making of an offer to the fiduciary in the United States.
4. "Substantial U.S. Market Interest" or "SUSMI": present with respect to a class of equity securities if (I) U.S. securities exchanges and NASDAQ in the aggregate constituted the single largest market for such class of securities in the issuer's prior fiscal year, or (ii) 20% or more of trading in the class of equity securities during such period occurred in such U.S. markets and less than 55% of trading in such securities took place during that period through the facilities of the securities markets or a single foreign country.
5. Separate SUSMI rules apply in the case of debt securities.
6. A "foreign issuer" is a foreign organized entity other than such an entity that has more than 50 percent of its voting securities being held by U.S. residents and either (I) the business of the company is administered principally in the U.S., (ii) 50 percent or more of its directors or executive officers are U.S. residents or (iii) more than 50% of its assets are located in the United States.
7. "Overseas Directed Offering": An offering by a foreign issuer "directed into a single country other than the United States to the residents thereof ... in accordance

with the local laws and customary practices and documentation of such country...."

8. "Offering Restrictions": Offering restrictions require each distributor to agree in writing that all offers and sales of the securities prior to the expiration of the distribution compliance period (A) shall be made only (I) in accordance with the provisions of the applicable safe harbors, (ii) pursuant to registration of the securities under the Securities Act, or (iii) pursuant to an available exemption from the registration requirements of the Securities Act and (B) for offers and sales of equity securities of domestic issuers not to engage in certain prohibited hedging transactions prior to the end of the distribution compliance period. The offering restrictions also require that all offering materials and documents (other than press releases) used in connection with offers and sales of the securities prior to the expiration of the distribution compliance period must include statements to the effect that the securities have not been registered under the Securities Act and may not be offered or sold in the United States or to U.S. Persons (other than distributors) unless the securities are registered under the Securities Act or an exemption from the registration requirements of the Securities Act is available, and, in the case of equity offerings by domestic issuers, statements concerning the hedging prohibition. Such statements should appear (I) on the cover or inside cover page of any prospectus or offering circular used in connection with the offer or sale of the securities, (ii) in the underwriting section of any prospectus or offering circular used in connection with the offer or sale of the securities, and (iii) in any advertisement made or issued by the issuer, any distributor, any of their respective affiliates, or any person acting on behalf of any of the foregoing. Such statements may appear in a summary form on prospectus cover pages and in advertisements.

9. Broker-dealers must ensure that they are not

unlawfully effecting distributions of Canadian securities in the United States in violation of Regulation S and other U.S. securities law requirements. This may result, for example, from purchases of small cap issues by foreign accounts from the issuer, a promoter or affiliated entities ostensibly using Regulation S or some other purported exemption for resale into the United States for the purpose of effecting a distribution. Such transactions may be found to violate the registration requirements of the Securities Act and have severe consequences.

This above information is for informational purposes only and should not be construed as legal advice or legal opinions on any specific facts or circumstances.

Chapter 10: Sample Regulation S Disclaimer Language

"Access to this website is restricted to persons who are not U.S. citizens and who are located outside of the U.S., pursuant to Regulation S under the U.S. Securities Act of 1933, as amended (the "Securities Act"). Nothing in this web site shall be deemed to constitute an offer, offer to sell, or the solicitation of an offer to buy, any securities in any U.S. jurisdiction.

"Each person accessing this web site will be deemed to have understood and agreed that: (1) he is not a U.S. citizen and he is located outside of the U.S; (2) any securities described herein have not been and will not be registered under the Securities Act or with any securities regulatory authority of any state, and may not be transferred to any U.S. citizen unless the securities are registered under the Securities Act, or an exemption from the registration requirements of the Securities Act is available.

"Each person accessing this web site acknowledges that hedging transactions involving securities offered and sold in accordance with Regulation S under the Securities Act may not be conducted unless in compliance with the Securities Act.

"If you accept the foregoing terms and the Terms of Use for this website, please select "Accept" below. Otherwise, press "Decline" to return to the previous page.

"As defined Regulation S under the Securities Act, the term "U.S person" means: (1) any natural person resident in the United States; (2) any partnership or corporation organized or incorporated under the laws of the United States; (3) any estate of which any executor or administrator is a U.S. person; (4) any trust of which any trustee is a U.S. person; (5) any agency or branch of a foreign entity located in the United States; (6) any non-discretionary account or similar account (other than an estate or trust) held by a dealer or other fiduciary for the benefit or account of a U.S. person; (7) any discretionary account or similar account (other than an estate or trust) held by a dealer or other fiduciary organized, incorporated, or (if an individual) resident in the United States; and (8) any partnership or corporation if: (A) organized or incorporated under the laws of any foreign jurisdiction; and (B) formed by a U.S. person principally for the purpose of investing in securities not registered under the Securities Act, unless it is organized or incorporated, and owned, by accredited investors (as defined in Rule 501(a) of the Securities Act) who are not natural persons.

www.ingramcontent.com/pod-product-compliance
Lightning Source LLC
Chambersburg PA
CBHW070958180526
45168CB00003B/1193